My Body

My Digestive System

Sally Hewitt

Library of Congress Control Number:
2008011710.

ISBN 978 1 59566 555 3

Printed and bound in China

Author Sally Hewitt
Consultant Terry Jennings
Project Editor Judith Millidge
Designer Kim Hall
Picture Researcher Claudia Tate
Illustrator Chris Davidson

Publisher Steve Evans
Creative Director Zeta Davies

Picture credits
Key: t = top, b = bottom, m = middle,
l =left, r = right

Alamy Bubbles Photolibrary 11r
Corbis Anna Peisl/zefa 21r
Getty Ryan McVay 8l, Seymour Hewitt 12, Camille
Tokerud 14, Tim Hall 16r, Atsuko Murano/ailead 21r
Shutterstock Jaimie Duplass 5, Olga Lyubkina 6, 7t, 15,
Matka Wariatka 7b, Andi Berger 9, Juriah Mosin 10,
Herbert Kratky 11, Elena Elisseeva 13, Vladimir Melnikov
17, Lorraine Kourafas 20

Words in bold are explained in the glossary on page 22.

Contents

What is your digestive system?

When you eat, your food goes on a journey through your **digestive system**.

On the way, your body takes nutrients (the bits that are good for you) from the food. Then, your body gets rid of the bits it can't use.

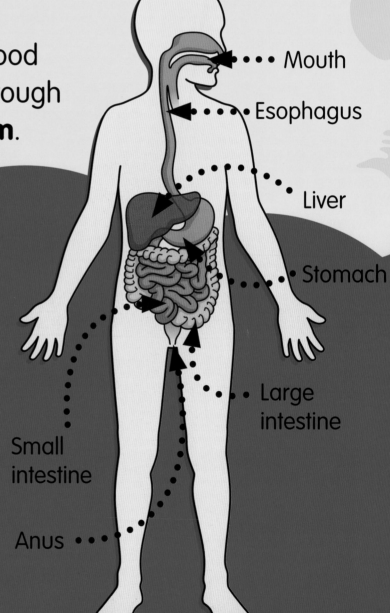

Mouth

Esophagus

Liver

Stomach

Large intestine

Small intestine

Anus

The journey is 21 feet long and takes about two days. The longest part of your digestive system is the small intestine. It is all curled up inside you.

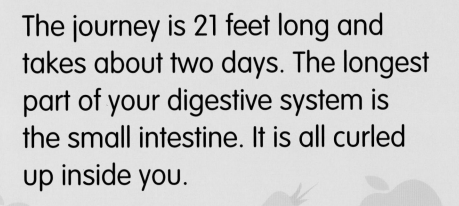

Activity

You need a ball of string and some scissors. Use the string to measure 20 lengths of a big shoe. Cut the string and stretch it out. That's about how far your food travels!

Food

Food gives you the **energy** you need to work and grow. It also helps you to keep warm and healthy. You need to eat something from each of these different food groups every day.

Fish, meat, eggs, and nuts help your body to grow and **heal**.

Bread, cereal, and pasta give you the energy you need to keep you going all day.

Milk, cheese, butter, and cream help to build strong bones and give you energy.

Fruit and vegetables are full of **vitamins** and **minerals** that help to keep you healthy. They are full of fiber, the rough part of food that helps your body to get rid of waste.

You only need a little sugar and salt in your food, but it is important to drink plenty of water.

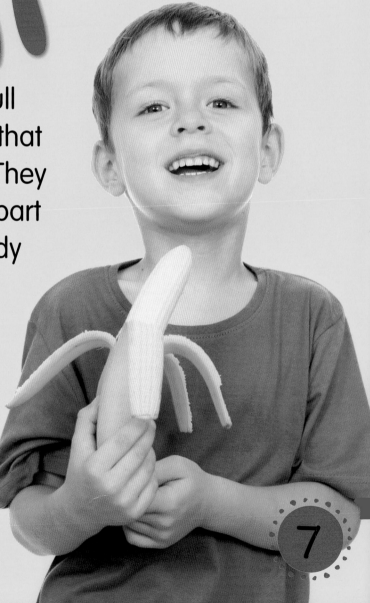

7

Mouth

Your food begins its journey in your mouth.

Seeing and smelling delicious food makes you want to eat. When you put food in your mouth, you taste its flavor with the tiny taste buds on your tongue.

Activity

Smell your favorite dinner cooking. Feel your mouth water. It is filling with saliva ready for eating!

8

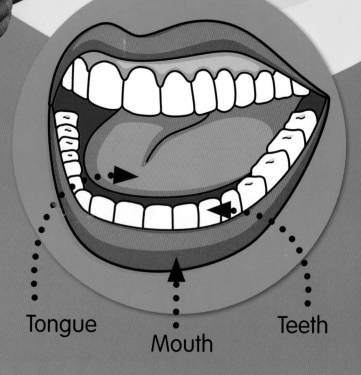

Tongue

Mouth

Teeth

You chew your food into small pieces with your teeth. Your front teeth are for biting. Your back teeth are for chewing.

Look after your teeth. You need them for eating!

Saliva helps to make your food slippery so you can swallow it easily. Your tongue helps you to swallow your food.

9

Esophagus

When you swallow a mouthful of chewed-up food, it goes down a tube called the esophagus (say *ee-sof-agus*). Your esophagus is next to your windpipe, which carries air to your lungs.

A little flap over your windpipe stops food going down it.

If you eat too fast and you cough, we say your food has "gone down the wrong way." That means, it has gone down your windpipe by mistake! Try to eat slowly to avoid choking!

Your food doesn't slither straight down into your stomach. Muscles in your esophagus squeeze it down slowly.

When giraffes bend down to drink, muscles in their esophagus push the water upwards!

If you eat bad food, your body gets rid of it. Muscles squeeze the food back up again and you are sick.

Being sick or vomiting feels horrible, but it helps you to get better quickly.

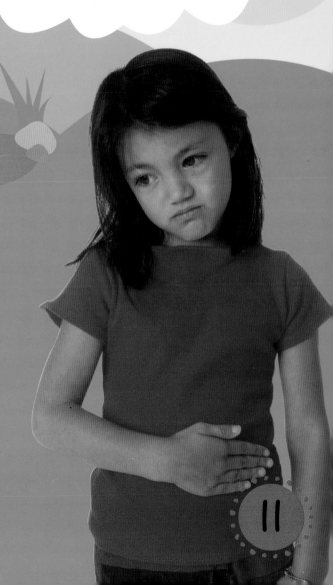

Stomach

Your esophagus pushes food into your stomach. Your stomach is a muscle. It is like a stretchy bag. It stretches when it is full of food.

Food stays in your stomach for about three hours while it is digested. 'Digested' means that it is mixed and mashed up.

After a big meal, you feel full up.

When your food has turned soft and runny like soup, it leaves your stomach. You start to feel **hungry** again when your stomach is empty.

Activity

Make a timetable of your meals. Notice the time when you feel hungry. Is it about three hours after your last meal? A healthy snack can stop you feeling hungry between meals.

Breakfast	8 o'clock
Lunch	1 o'clock
Supper	6 o'clock

Small intestine

Your food takes about four hours to ooze along your small intestine where it becomes even more runny and watery. Bubbles of gas in your intestines make a rumbling sound while your food is being digested.

Activity

Listen to tummy rumbles. When a friend's or one of your family's tummy rumbles loudly, ask if you can put your ear on their stomach and listen to their food being digested!

14

Food is full of "nutrients" or goodness that your body needs to grow, to keep healthy, and to provide you with energy. While your food is in your small intestine, nutrients from your food go into your blood.

It's important to eat food full of the nutrients your body needs.

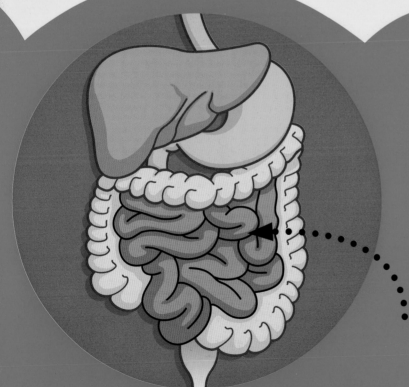

Your small intestine is longer than your large intestine. It is called small because it is narrow.

Small intestine

15

Liver and blood

Blood full of nutrients from your food goes to your liver. Your liver is the biggest organ in your body.

Your liver makes a special juice called bile, which breaks down food into things the body can use. It stores the nutrients and gets rid of the parts of food that are bad for you.

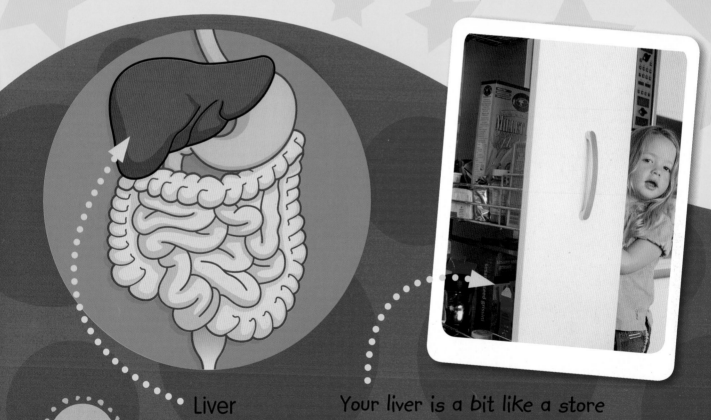

Liver

Your liver is a bit like a store cupboard. It gives you some food for now and stores some for later.

When your liver has done its job, it sends nutrients into your blood through your blood vessels.

Your blood delivers goodness from your food to every bit of your body.

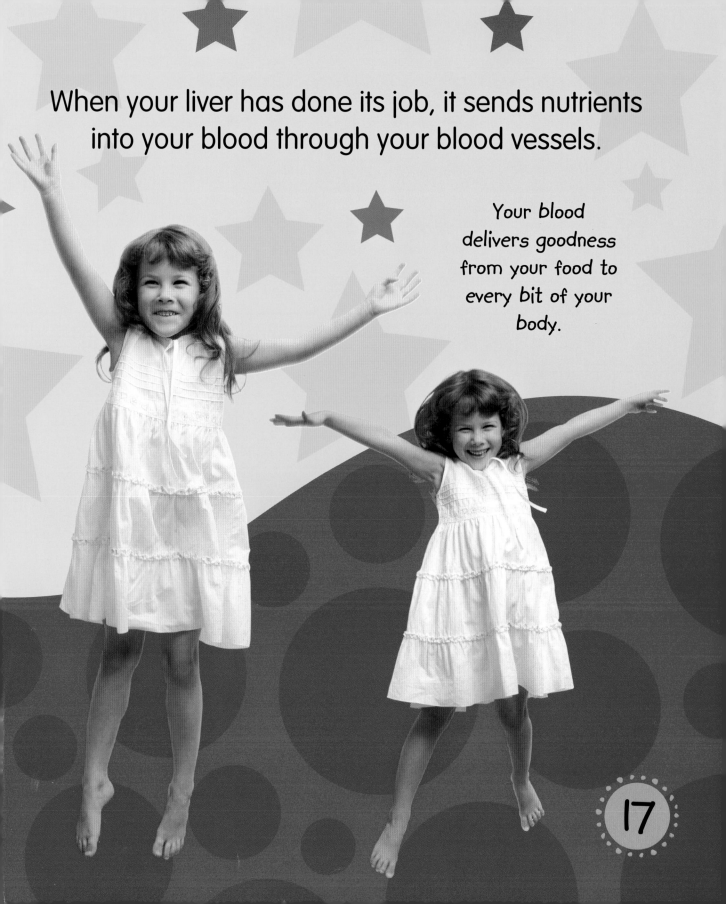

17

Large intestine

When your food reaches the large intestine, it is mostly waste. Waste is the part of your food that your body doesn't need. It goes into the large intestine and stays there for about two days.

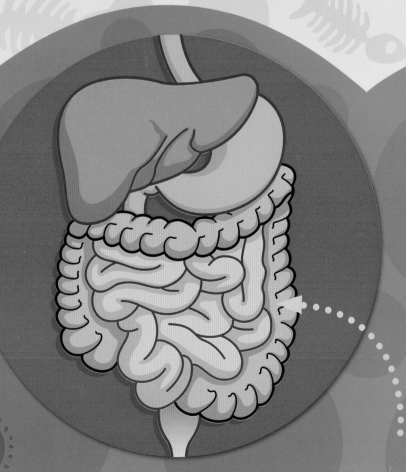

While your food is in your large intestine, the last little bit of nutrients and most of the water goes into your body. Your food is nearly at the end of its journey.

Large intestine

By the time the remains of your food reach the end of your large intestine, it has become "feces." Your body gets rid of feces through an opening called the anus.

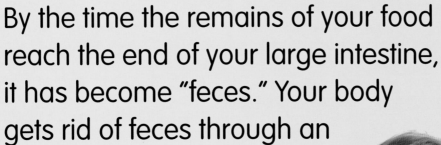

Poo is what is left of your food after the goodness has been taken from it.

19

Healthy digestive system

There are lots of ways you can keep your digestive system healthy.

- Eat healthy food full of the nutrients your body needs.

- Drink plenty of water. Water helps food go through your digestive system.

Drink water with a meal, when you are thirsty. Drink a bit more when it's hot or you are exercising.

Try to eat lots of fruit and vegetables. They are delicious and help to make you strong and healthy.

Fruit and vegetables are full of fiber.

Activity

Start the day with a breakfast that is good for your digestive system. Wash and grate an apple including the peel. Slice a banana. Add milk, a little lemon juice, honey and a sprinkle of oats. Mix it all together and eat up!

Glossary

Digestion
When your body digests food, it mashes it up, uses the goodness and gets rid of the waste.

Digestive system
Your digestive system is all the parts of your body that work together to digest your food.

Energy
Energy is what you need to give you the power to work. Food gives you energy.

Heal
Your body heals or gets better when you cut yourself or when you are ill.

Hungry
You feel hungry when your stomach is empty. Feeling hungry makes you want to eat.

Minerals
Minerals are tiny parts of goodness in food. Minerals in milk help you build strong teeth and bones.

Saliva
Saliva is a liquid like water in your mouth. It helps you to taste and swallow your food.

Vitamins
Vitamins are tiny parts of goodness in food. Vitamins in fruit help to keep your skin healthy.

Notes for parents and teachers

1. Explain that we are a kind of animal called a human and that all animals need food and drink to stay alive. Find pictures of different animals and look at the food they eat.

2. Talk about how we all need energy to give us the power to work and play, and that food gives us energy. Discuss other kinds of energy, such as gasoline for cars, and electricity for light. What happens to us without food, to a car without gasoline and to a light without electricity?

3. Put out a variety of food and sort it into the main food groups (see pages 6 and 7). Discuss what is the same about the food in each group and talk about why your body needs each different kind of food.

4. Explain why it is so important to keep our teeth healthy. Eat a piece of crusty bread together. Point out how your front teeth bite, the pointed teeth tear, and the back teeth chew. Notice how they are the right shape for the job they do. Talk about the kind of food we would have to eat if we didn't have teeth!

5. Draw a simple picture of the digestive system together (see page 4). Trace the route your food takes. Name each part the food is going through and describe what is happening to the food. Use words such as chew, swallow, mix, and mash.

23

Index